PUBLISHED BY
PRINCETON ARCHITECTURAL PRESS
A MCEVOY GROUP COMPANY
202 WARREN STREET, HUDSON, NY 12534
VISIT OUR WEBSITE AT WWW.PAPRESS.COM

FIRST PUBLISHED IN FRANCE UNDER THE TITLE *DU MATIN AU SOIR*
ⓒ 2016 HÉLIUM / ACTES SUD, PARIS, FRANCE

EDITOR: NICOLA BROWER / TYPESETTING: MIA JOHNSON

SPECIAL THANKS TO: JANET BEHNING, NOLAN BOOMER, ABBY BUSSEL,
BARBARA DARKO, BENJAMIN ENGLISH, JENNY FLORENCE, JAN CIGLIANO HARTMAN,
SUSAN HERSHBERG, LIA HUNT, VALERIE KAMEN, SIMONE KAPLAN–SENCHAK,
JENNIFER LIPPERT, SARA MCKAY, ELIANNA MILLER, WES SEELEY, ROB SHAEFFER,
SARA STEMEN, PAUL WAGNER, AND JOSEPH WESTON OF
PRINCETON ARCHITECTURAL PRESS —KEVIN C. LIPPERT, PUBLISHER

LIBRARY OF CONGRESS CATALOGING–IN–PUBLICATION DATA
AVAILABLE FROM THE PUBLISHER.

flavia ruotolo

from morning

to night

A BOOK OF HIDDEN SHAPES

PRINCETON ARCHITECTURAL PRESS · NEW YORK

a morning meal

a magic mushroom

an orange

a planet

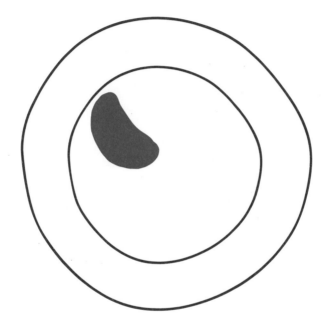

a segment

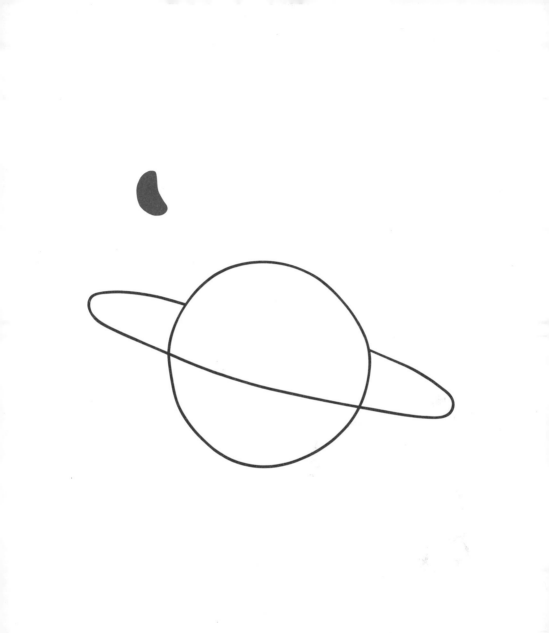

an orbit

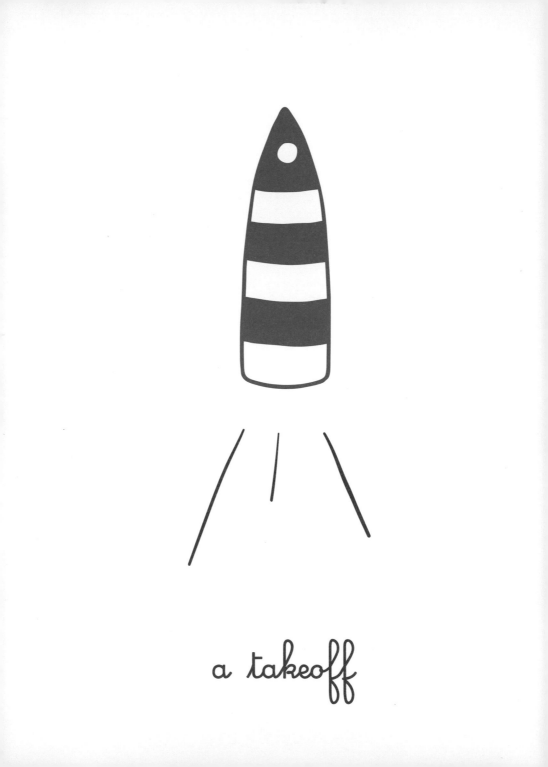

a takeoff

a gust of wind

an assignment

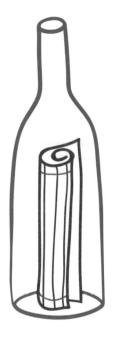

a message

a surprise

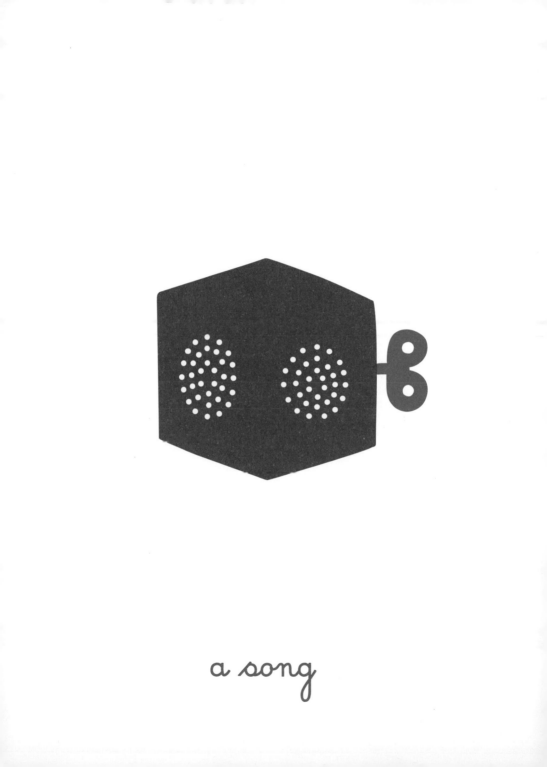

a song

a lesson

an invention

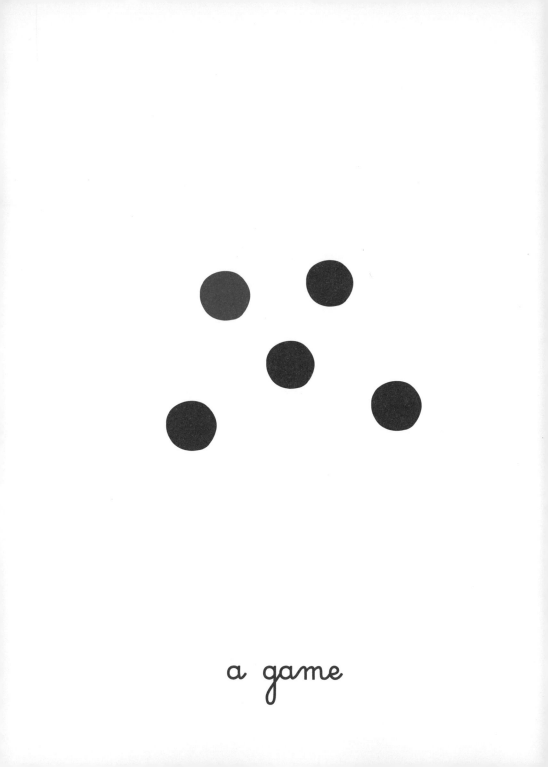

a game

a cloudy afternoon

a path

the night sky

a direction

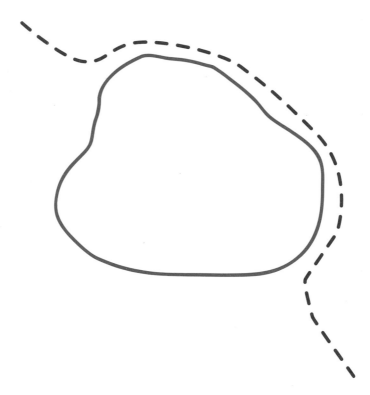

an obstacle

a treasure

disappointment

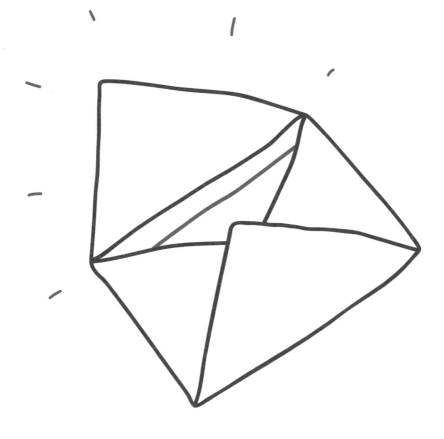

delight

the letter U

a horseshoe

a donkey, a dog,
a cat, a rooster

a fairy tale

a moon landing

a sunset

a story read . . .

...time for bed

Flavia Ruotolo
was born in 1973. After
studying experimental animation
and film in Bologna and Paris, she
worked as a video designer for television.
She became interested in graphic design
and illustration and opened her own
studio, Le Macchinine, where she
specializes in designs for children.
Her first book, Zoo, was published
in French in 2011 by
MéMo.